The Integrity
of Preaching

The James A. Gray Fund was established at the Divinity School of Duke University in 1946 as a part of the Methodist College Advance of North Carolina conferences of the Methodist Church. The purpose of the fund, in the words of the donor, is to expand and maintain the educational services of Duke Divinity School in "behalf of North Carolina churches and pastors, particularly rural churches and pastors."

The Integrity
of Preaching

JOHN KNOX

Lectures on the James A. Gray Fund of the Divinity School
of Duke University, Durham, North Carolina

ABINGDON PRESS
New York • Nashville

THE INTEGRITY OF PREACHING

Copyright © MCMLVII by Abingdon Press

Library of Congress Catalog Card Number: 57-5279

Scripture quotations unless otherwise noted are from the
Revised Standard Version of the Bible and are copyright 1946
and 1952 by the Division of Christian Education of the National Council of the Churches of Christ in the U.S.A.

SET UP, PRINTED, AND BOUND BY THE
PARTHENON PRESS, AT NASHVILLE,
TENNESSEE, UNITED STATES OF AMERICA

FOREWORD

OF ALL THE MANY ABLE AND FAITHFUL PREACHERS OF
the gospel who, usually without intending it, have been
my teachers in homiletics, the one who has meant im-
measurably more to me than any other is my own father,
Absalom Knox, who died just over thirty years ago. Although he spent his days in obscure places, he was a
great preacher (in the only sense in which that term
ought ever to be used) and, had not death cut him
down in the midst of his years, would have become a
greater one. He had not the advantage of a full college
course, much less of seminary training, but he was one
of the most intelligent, sensitive, and humane persons I
have ever known, and therefore one of the best educated.
He was a wonderfully good man and was recognized as
such by all who knew him; but he was also a vivid and
passionate person and had gifts of authentic eloquence
only rarely found.

But when I think of him as a preacher, I do not think
first of these gifts, but of the seriousness with which he
took his preaching and the absolute honesty with which
he did it, the long and careful work he devoted to pre-

paring for it (all of us knew that for the first few hours of each day we must not "disturb Father"), the biblical quality of it, its solidity and wholeness, the way it answered to the life of the church, the way it spoke to the heart. It was the memory of his preaching more than anything else which suggested the word "integrity" for the title of these reflections of my own about the preacher and his work.

In writing Chapter II, I drew freely upon an essay of my own, "Authenticity and Relevance," published several years ago in *The Union Seminary Review*.

I am grateful to Dean James Cannon of the Divinity School of Duke University and his colleagues for the invitation to give the Gray Lectures there in June of 1956 and for the many courtesies they showed me during the period of the lectures. I also want to thank my beloved friend Paul Scherer for reading my manuscript and giving me many helpful criticisms.

JOHN KNOX

CONTENTS

7

Chapter I

When Is Preaching Biblical?

WE ARE WITNESSING IN OUR DAY A FRESH INSISTENCE that preaching shall be biblical. Nothing is more characteristic of contemporary discussions of preaching than this emphasis. The preacher's message must be derived, not from current events or current literature or current trends of one sort or another, not from the philosophers, the statesmen, or the poets, not even, in the last resort, from the preacher's own experience or reflection, but from the Scriptures. There is, of course, nothing really new about this. That it needs to be said again, and with fresh emphasis, means only that preaching has departed in this respect from its own tradition. What we are strenuously asserting other ages have taken for granted. Preaching in the early centuries and preaching in all the most vital and creative periods of the church's history has been biblical preaching.

But *when* is preaching biblical? Preachers use the Bible, and have always used it, in a great variety of ways. Not all preaching which takes the form of biblical exposition can be called biblical preaching in any appreciative or really authentic sense. Indeed, as we know quite well,

9

biblical exposition itself can be very barren and dull—
and therefore (do we dare say?) very unbiblical. In one of
the books of William Law, the eighteenth century
English mystic, there is a charming story of a kind
woman's gift of a biblical commentary to an old shepherd
named John and his wife Betty. The shepherd describes
what happened:

Madam, the Squire's wife, of our Town, hearing how Betty
and I loved the Scriptures, brought us one day a huge expounding book upon the New Testament; and told us
that we should understand the Scriptures a deal better by
reading it in that book than in the New Testament alone. . . .
The next Lord's Day, when two or three Neighbors according to custom came to sit with us in the evening, "Betty,"
said I, "bring out Madam's great book and read the fifth
chapter of St. Matthew." When she had done that, I bid
her read the fifteenth chapter of the First Epistle to the
Corinthians. The next morning said I to Betty, "Carry this
great expounding book again to my mistress and tell her that
the words of Christ, and His Apostles, are best by themselves,
and just as they left them." And as I was that morning going
to my sheep, thought I to myself, This great expounding
book seems to have done just as much good to this little
book of the New Testament by being added to it, and mixed
with it, as a Gallon of water would do to a little cup of true
wine by being added to it or mixed with it. The wine indeed
would be all there; but its fine taste and cordial spirit which
it had when drunk by itself would be all lost and drowned
in the coldness and deadness of the water.[1]

Preachers will probably take a particular delight in this
story, and it is only natural that they should, because

they have had to suffer perhaps more than others from uninspired and unenlightening commentators. But let us remember that the preacher is also an expositor and that a sermon can hide or distort a biblical text as certainly and as thoroughly as any commentary. It is not the scholars' "huge expounding books" alone about which it can sometimes be said that they succeed only in dulling "the fine taste" of the original and diluting its "cordial spirit"; the preachers' long expounding discourses often have the same effect. In other words, making use—even large use—of the Bible is not enough to guarantee effective, or even authentic, biblical preaching. Everything depends on how we make use of it.

We shall devote several of these chapters to a discussion of this "how"; but first perhaps something more should be said about the "why." For it is the grounds for using the Bible at all in preaching which largely determine how our actual ways of using it should be judged. I suggest that these grounds can be summarily indicated in some such way as this: We use the Bible in preaching because it is great literature, because it is our literature, and because it is, in a very true and distinctive sense, God's literature. These reasons stand in an order of ascending importance, but each deserves some attention.

Certainly one reason why it is appropriate to use the Bible in preaching, and why we do in fact use it, is that it is great religious literature. Perhaps we do not need to use the second adjective since there is a sense in which all great literature may be said to be "religious." Innumerable attempts have been made—and by persons much more competent than I to make them—to define "great"

11

literature, to say just what a great book is. It is fair to say that none of these attempts has perfectly succeeded. The criteria of great art cannot be precisely and exhaustively formulated. We know the great book in the way we know great music—by the way we permanently respond to it, by what it does and continues to do to us—and the only objective check upon our impression of it is the response of others. The great literature of the world is composed of the books about which many men and women in many generations find themselves saying, "This is a great book!" It is certainly safe to say that such books will always deal, not with abstract conceptions merely nor yet with fancies, but with human experience in its concreteness and existential truth. They will search out the deep things in man, the sources of his greatness and of his tragic failure. They will set him in a large place, imparting some sense of the ultimate meaning, the mystery, of his life. And they will do all of this through the medium of language which is simple, clear, and moving. But however we try to formulate our definition of great literature, there is no doubt that the Bible as a whole and many parts of it when taken separately fully qualify as such. It is not only great literature, but it is in some respects incomparably great. It is the most realistic, profound, and moving account of man which man has produced. But preaching is also profoundly, radically, concerned with man, his need and his redemption, and it is no more effective, or even more genuine, than the preacher's understanding of the human situation is deep, and sure, and true. The Bible provides superb resources for this understanding. For this reason, if for no other, the preacher will find himself using it.

But a more potent reason for our use of the Bible in preaching is that it is our literature. I mean, of course, that it is the literature of the church. The books of the Old Testament (or at least those of the Law and the Prophets) were in familiar and constant use among Jews for centuries before the same books were adopted by the Christian community. These writings have from the very earliest times been associated with the life of the church, and associated with it in the most significant and intimate fashion. Jesus knew and quoted from these books; so of course did Paul. His own letters and other specifically Christian documents, especially the Gospels which described Jesus' career and recorded his words, were soon to be accorded the same high status and to enjoy the same familiar use. For twenty centuries the church—indeed the whole of Christendom—has been nourished on these ancient writings. Biblical images and conceptions have entered into the warp and woof of Western culture; the language of the Bible not only has been the basic ingredient in the language of the church's liturgy and devotion, but it has also profoundly affected our general literature and our common speech. Now the songs our mothers taught us were probably good songs, but it is not their intrinsic goodness alone that makes them precious to us. We love them, less perhaps because of anything they contain in and of themselves, than because our mothers, and probably their mothers also, loved them. In the same way the Bible has acquired a heightened meaning and value from the church's use

13

of it. Such passages as the twenty-third psalm, the first few verses of the fifth chapter of Romans, or certain sayings of Jesus in the Gospels have acquired values they could not have had when they were first spoken or written. A familiar biblical phrase can sometimes evoke a whole world of remembered, or half-remembered, meanings. Indeed, some of the deepest of these meanings can scarcely be evoked in any other way. But it is just such meanings—concrete, existential meanings— that preaching is seeking to communicate. No wonder it uses the Bible! How could it help doing so?

But the third reason is the really decisive one: It is God's literature. It is, as we say, "the Word of God." If it could not be called the Word of God, not only is it highly doubtful that it would be used in preaching, but also that it would be familiarly used at all—or even that there would be such a thing as preaching. If men had not found, and did not find still, in the history that began with Abraham and culminated in Christ, and in the communal life which belonged to this history, or to which this history belonged (one can look at the relationship both ways)—if men had not found there the very presence and the mighty action of God, there would be neither church, Bible, nor preaching. It is not because the Bible is made up of, or contains, God's words (as though God spoke words at all) that we call it the Word of God, but because it conveys to us this presence and this mighty action. Now Christian preaching is attempting to convey this same presence and this same mighty action. It, like the Bible itself, is concerned with the event of Christ, seeking to communicate its

14

reality and its relevance, to interpret its meaning for the men of every generation and for man in all the generations. The Bible, therefore, is not merely useful in preaching; it is absolutely indispensable. It is more than a supremely useful resource in preaching; it belongs essentially to the very source of preaching. It is not only true that preaching *should* be biblical; authentic preaching has to be!

But, we ask again, what *is* biblical preaching? Now enough has been said to indicate that one cannot define biblical preaching in terms of any mechanical or external or merely formal connection between the Bible and the sermon. One cannot say, for example, that biblical preaching is simply preaching from a biblical text. I can remember hearing when I was in seminary of a distinction between topical and textual sermons. That may be a useful distinction for certain purposes, but it will not do to regard all textual sermons as biblical and all topical sermons as unbiblical. It is possible, we all know, to take a biblical text and proceed to preach a very unbiblical sermon. One may do this in several ways. One of these is to quote a few words of scripture as a kind of ornamental frontispiece for a discourse which really owes nothing either to these words or to any part of scripture. I remember, for example, several times years ago hearing—and I confess with shame, once preaching—a sermon of this kind (first preached, so far as I can discover, by Charles Reynolds Brown) on the question once asked Jacob by Pharaoh, "How old are you?" (Gen. 47:8)—a sermon on "the dimensions of life." In that

15

case, and in innumerable similar ones, any connection between the sermon and anything the Bible is really interested in saying is purely accidental. Or one can take a text and then misinterpret it, as when one uses "Search the Scriptures," the King James Version translation of John 5:39, as a text for a sermon on the duty of Bible reading. Or one may take out of the Bible a quite unbiblical text—that is, a verse or two which are not typical or representative—and then deal with them, closely and faithfully enough perhaps, but without reference to what the Bible as a whole is saying. In a word, preaching from a text, or even what we call expository preaching, is not as such biblical preaching.

Nor can biblical preaching be defined as preaching which has the Bible as its subject or which relies on the Bible for much of its subject matter. Carl S. Patton, in his book *The Use of the Bible in Preaching*, seems to take for granted that by biblical preaching we mean preaching *about* the Bible. He writes, for example:

I do not maintain that all preaching should be biblical. Far from it. Religion is in the making, all the time. Current happenings in political, economic and international life call aloud for comment and for Christian interpretation by the Christian prophet. Contemporary scientific and philosophical thought moves constantly on, with new bearings upon religious beliefs and practices. It is idle to pretend that the only things we need to talk about in the pulpit are to be found in the Bible.*

* This and the following quotations are from *The Use of the Bible in Preaching*. Copyright 1936 by Harper & Brothers and used by their permission. It is recognized that the quotations do not fairly represent the entire book, which has many merits.

The idea seems to be that preaching can either be biblical and deal with the Bible or else relevant and deal with what is actually going on in the world—but not both. (About this fallacy something will be said in the next chapter.)

Patton's story of how he got started on "biblical" preaching is almost as lively and entertaining as his sermons must have been:

But one time, perhaps fifteen or twenty years ago, I tried a biblical sermon. I suppose I did it because nobody had been killed that week who needed to be preached about, and nothing had happened in Japan or Italy or the League of Nations that required my elucidation, and I was pressed for a topic. I had been reading the old story of the Tower of Babel. So in a moment of hardihood—or perhaps of desperation—I said to myself, "I'll make a sermon out of that." I felt rather apologetic about it. Why drag my modern, up-to-the-minute people back to that far-off, long past and unfinished tower? But I couldn't think of anything else that week, and it had to do. To my astonishment, the comments on that sermon almost led me to suppose that the people of my congregation had been lying awake nights wondering about that old story.

Patton gives us hardly more than a hint of the actual content of this first "biblical" sermon. He is more explicit in his description of his second attempt:

I tried it again. I took about the most unlikely piece of homiletical material to be found in the entire Old Testament: the fifth chapter of Genesis. I went at it somewhat realistically. I inquired how these old gentlemen came to live so long, and what was wrong with modern medicine and hygiene that we could not compete with them. I asked how they amused themselves after they got to be five or six hundred years old. I raised the question whether they were ever sick, and, if they were, whether they had arthritis (I suppose it would have been rheumatism in their time) for ten or fifteen years as people do nowadays, or for a couple of hundred years. I asked whether the women lived as long as the men, and at what age any of them were supposed to be grown up and fit to go out by themselves without their fathers or mothers. Then I told quite frankly what sort of story I thought it was: not history, but a lovely piece of folklore in which the Hebrews of a later time had pictured a golden age long past when a man was still a boy at fifty, in his prime at somewhere around six or seven hundred, and began to feel the approach of old age as he drew near the nine hundred mark. This seemed to be news to the people. And they seemed much interested in it. In fact this particular sermon was requested by and printed in the journal of one of our theological schools.[2]

It is only fair to say that Patton adds: "If such preaching were only interesting, that would not carry us far enough. But this kind of preaching is informative—educative—in two ways." But as one reads on, one finds that both of these "ways" have largely to do with people's coming to have more intelligent ideas about the Bible itself.

For defects in understanding which we may find exhibited in this lively book of Patton's we will not blame the particular writer. We shall recognize the quoted passages as being fairly representative of the theological climate in sections of Protestantism a generation ago.

18

But they also serve to remind us that biblical preaching cannot be defined merely as preaching which is explicitly and largely concerned with biblical materials —no matter what the materials are or how they are dealt with. As a matter of fact, the difference between biblical and unbiblical preaching has little to do with the structure of the sermon and whether it is topical or expository in form. The difference lies deeper than that. If it is possible, as we have been saying, to preach a quite unbiblical sermon on a biblical text, it is also possible to preach a quite biblical sermon on no text at all.

How then can we define biblical preaching? Much of the rest of this book will be seeking to answer this question, and no real attempt will be made here. Let us briefly make four points which cannot be sharply separated from one another. First, we may say that biblical preaching is preaching which remains close to the characteristic and essential biblical ideas: the transcendence, the holiness, the power and sovereignty, the love of God; his demand of ethical righteousness; his judgment upon sin; man's creaturehood, his plight as a sinner; his need of forgiveness and release; the meaning of Christ as the actual coming of God into our history with the help we need; the availability of reconciliation and redemption, of life, joy, and peace, in the new community of the Spirit which God created through Christ and into which we can enter upon the sole condition of penitence and faith. And in biblical preaching such ideas will appear not as mere ideas—not as broad general conceptions only—but rather in the concrete context of the church's tradition and life. Biblical preaching is not concerned with abstractions. It was "existentialist" long before the philosophers began to use that word. Indeed, it is not an accident that Kierkegaard, the father of modern existentialism, was a biblical preacher.

Secondly, biblical preaching is preaching which is centrally concerned with the central biblical event, the event of Christ. The mere treating of incidents in the biblical narrative or scraps of teaching, even when done faithfully and in an edifying manner, does not qualify preaching as biblical unless the incidents and teachings are seen and presented in their relation to God's total act of redemption which culminated in the life and death of Jesus, the Resurrection, the coming of the Spirit, and the creation of the church. Sinclair Lewis, in *Babbitt*, has some satirical comments to make on the various lectures on "philosophy and Oriental ethnology" which were being delivered by "earnest spinsters" in the several classrooms of a Sunday school. Discussions of biblical materials will be precisely such lectures (whether informed or uninformed, whether dull like those Lewis has in mind or interesting, even amusing, like those Patton sometimes gives us), or else they will be mere moralistic and probably sentimental exhortations, unless they are primarily concerned with setting forth the meaning of God's new relation with men as brought about through the event and as embodied in the church.

The very word "preach" should remind us of this primary purpose and character of preaching. The original English form of the word was *prechen*, derived immediately from the Old French *prechier* (the modern *prêcher*), and ultimately from the Latin *praedico*, which means to declare in public, to proclaim, to publish. It is often supposed that this Latin term answers to the Greek *prophēteuo*, to prophesy. But *prophēteuo* and *prophēteia*, as they appear in the New Testament, are regularly transliterated in the Latin versions, appearing as *propheto* and *prophetia*. *Praedico* translates *kērusso*, and *praedicatio*, *kērugma*; and these words, Greek as well as Latin, denote a public declaration, a proclamation, indeed an announcement in the simple, most general, sense. The *kērux* was a herald; and *kērugma* was the news he brought. Since the news is good news, the New Testament prefers *evangelion* to *kērugma*. The preacher is the herald of the good news. He proclaims the acceptable year of the Lord. Preaching, as the function is developed in the church, is, to be sure, more than the simple proclamation. Although the Latin *praedico* renders only the one Greek term *kērusso*, the actual work of preaching has come to include functions originally denoted by other terms, notably "prophecy" and "teaching." But the basic meaning of "preaching" is still announcing something that has happened; and the more complicated and inclusive meaning of the term can be truly understood only if that basic meaning is carried in mind. The preacher is still, first of all, a preacher of the gospel. His message is thus primarily determined by an ancient event—the event centering in the death and resurrection of Jesus Christ. Only such preaching is biblical.

In the third place, biblical preaching is preaching

21

which answers to and nourishes the essential life of the church. For the event which it proclaims is more than an ancient happening known to us only through the documentary accounts of it which happened to be written and have happened to survive. It issued in, and its true meaning is perpetuated in, the new community of the Spirit. Here is the reality of the Resurrection. The preacher is not repeating, over and over again, an ancient chronicle; he is bearing witness to the quality and significance of a new communal life in which God is making available to us a new health and salvation. His preaching is an ellipse moving about the two foci of the ancient event and the always new life of the Spirit. Since one can truly speak of the event only in the light of the continuing experience of the church and one can truly interpret the life of the church only in the light of the remembered event, the two foci tend to become a single center. But the true shape of preaching is an ellipse, not a circle, and the tension between the event and the Spirit is as important as their mutuality. Preaching fails as often because both are too easily identified as because either is simply ignored. To hold the two elements together in their full integrity and distinctive force, *but to hold them together*, is the basic problem of preaching.

Finally, biblical preaching will be preaching in which the event in a real sense is recurring. The God who acted in the events out of which the church arose acts afresh in the preacher's word. The preaching of the gospel is itself a part of the gospel. The true biblical preacher is not merely discussing events of the past (like a history professor), nor is he merely drawing edifying

22

lessons out of its life (like a moral guide or philosopher).
In his inspired words the past event is happening again.
True preaching is itself an event—and an event of a
particular kind. In it the revelation of God in Christ is
actually recurring. The eschatological event, which began
in the coming of Christ and will end with the final
judgment on, and fulfillment of, history, is taking place
recurrently or, if you prefer, continuously, in the sacraments and preaching of the church. If that is not true,
neither the sacraments nor the preaching matters much.
Indeed, if that is not true, sacraments and preaching, in
any authentic sense, do not exist at all.

The Christian Scriptures come to us directly out of
the life of the primitive church and have been conveyed
to us through the life of the church in all the centuries
since. Their principal value lies in the fact that they
bring us, in its concrete character, the event in which
the church began and which determined the church's
initial and essential nature. The Scriptures so answer
to the life of the primitive community in response to
this event as that in reading them we are ourselves
brought into touch with the event and enabled to
participate in the life. True biblical preaching is preaching which has this same effect in every age.

Chapter II

The Relevance of Biblical Preaching

TOWARD THE END OF THE PRECEDING CHAPTER, I SPOKE of preaching as having, so to speak, the shape of an ellipse about two foci, the ancient event and the always new life of the Spirit. More needs to be said about the integrity and distinctiveness of each of these concerns as well as about their essential mutuality.

In beginning an account of her religious experience, a woman writing in one of our national magazines a few years ago remarked that early in her career she turned from the church because it seemed to her to have too little contact with either the first century or the twentieth to be significant. I do not remember the title of her article or even her own name and can recall nothing as to the context of her statement or the general course of her argument or confession; but I have not forgotten the sting of that opening remark, the sharp decisiveness of her dismissal of the church. Can anyone deny that there is truth in her indictment? And who will dispute that, insofar as it is true, it is an absolutely damning indictment? Certainly, critics may argue, we have the right to expect that the church shall be in touch with reality somewhere: if not with our own century, then at least with the first; if not with the first, then by all means with the twentieth. Or to state the issue from the Christian's point of view, what could we say in justification of a Christianity—or of Christian preaching—that was both unbiblical and irrelevant?

I have emphasized the conjunctions "either" and "or" in the remark I have quoted, but I am not sure the writer would have wanted us to do so, and I am quite sure that doing so hides an important part of its significance. Such a reading suggests that it might be possible for the church to have contact with the first century or the twentieth without having contact with both, that it might be possible for preaching to be biblical without being relevant or to be relevant without being biblical. But that is not true. In this case, at least, relevance and historical authenticity are two sides of a single coin.

Consider, for example, the preacher who believes his preaching is in the closest contact with the first century—he is sure he is preaching the "true gospel"— when actually it lacks any touch with the twentieth. Is he not obviously mistaken about its connection with the first? Being in touch with the first century does not mean merely repeating the words of the first century or making frequent complimentary references to the first century; surely it means something like sharing the experience of the first century, knowing the sources of power it knew, possessing a common life with it. But a church cannot be in touch with the first century in this sense without being a living community; and a living community, in addition to being in organic relation with the life of the past, belongs organically within the life of its own period. Indeed, it is only in a living present that one can have any vital contact with the past, or that the past itself can be said still to exist. Being in touch with a living past is more than merely having had such a past; it is more than knowing one has had it or reminding oneself and others frequently that one has; it is actually being a living continuation of it.

But the same kind of thing can be said of the church which has no real connection with the first century but thinks it is in the most fruitful kind of relation with the twentieth. Such a church is mistaken in supposing that a society can be a church at all without sustaining a living contact with the first century and all the centuries since. It may be contemporaneous otherwise, but it is not a contemporaneous church. For the church has its distinctive character in any and every century in virtue of its relation to the events which happened in the first; and only in that character has it any relevant word to speak or any really apposite service to perform.

In a word, if we as preachers are not speaking to the needs of the contemporary world, it is a fair guess that we have not really heard the gospel of the early church. On the other hand, however much concern we may have about the contemporary world, that concern is not Christian except as it stems from the conviction that an event occurred in the first century in the light of which alone the meaning of the contemporary scene can be understood and in the power of which alone the community we seek can be realized. Only authentically biblical preaching can be really relevant; only vitally relevant preaching can be really biblical.

The recognition of this relationship between historical authenticity and relevance brings the biblical scholar and the biblical preacher much nearer together than they often seem to be and lays bare the common ground on which they stand if each is performing his proper function. The difference between them is not that one is concerned about historical truth and the other about contemporary value. They will both be concerned with both, although a difference in emphasis gives each a distinctive role.

Consider first the strictly historical approach—that is, the approach dominated by interest in the history for its own sake. Now the outer facts of the history can be established—or not, as the case may be—without any reference to relevance. But the inner meaning (and that is nothing less than the concrete reality) of the history can be grasped only by one who is sensitive to the meaning of his own time. There is a mutual relationship here, a kind of alternation or rhythm, the past throwing light on the present and the present on the past; but in some measure concern for relevance and concern for authenticity must be present throughout and from the start. The student of history must bring with him at least a capacity for deep understanding of the present if he is ever to achieve any deep understanding of the past. Herbert Butterfield's book *Christianity and History*[3] is a brilliant example of the truth of this. "It is almost

27

impossible," he writes at one point, "properly to appreciate the higher developments in the historical reflection of the Old Testament except in another age which has experienced (or has found itself confronted with) colossal cataclysm, an age like the one in which we live." And one might add that the more profoundly a particular historian feels the impact and meaning of the present cataclysm, the more profoundly authentic can be his understanding of what the prophets were trying to say. We are witnessing now a remarkable reawakening of interest in the Old Testament. We should make a mistake if we attributed this simply to the Dead Sea Scrolls or to the fact that there are just now so many brilliant scholars and teachers in that field. The prior and really decisive factor is the tragic history of our own times which has made the Old Testament freshly relevant and has therefore enabled first our professors and then us to hear with new understanding its authentic voice.

In the same way our understanding of the New Testament and of the events which created it depends, for its depth and truth, far more upon our capacity for insight into the meaning of our present existence than upon any technical equipment we may have for studying ancient documents or any amount of learning and lore —valuable, and for certain important purposes indispensable, as such qualifications undoubtedly are. Christ must live for us, must come within our existence, must find us where we are, if we are ever to know the wonder of the Incarnation or the power—and therefore the truth—of the Resurrection. Milner-White begins one of his prayers: "O Christ, whose wondrous birth mean-eth nothing unless we be born again, whose death and sacrifice nothing unless we die unto sin, whose resurrection nothing if thou be risen alone . . ." [4] Whatever can be said of history in general, there can be no authentic knowledge of the history to which the Christian looks back—what the Germans call the *Heilsgeschichte*—without this kind of participation; and one who in preoccupation with authenticity shuts out all considerations of relevance, ends by missing, not only relevance, but authenticity as well.

But the obverse is also true. Consider the case of the preacher who approaches the biblical history with an interest primarily in relevance. Such a one is in particular peril of becoming irrelevant. This is true because the relevance of the biblical history lies in considerable part in the challenge it presents to conventional assumptions and customary ways of thinking, whereas attention solely to relevance tends toward modernization and assimilation. The Bible is made to answer only our questions—that is, the questions we are *consciously* asking—and is prevented from answering the questions which are in the first instance its own but which, having been asked, prove to be our own deeper questions also. The points where the Bible is most relevant to the twentieth century are precisely the points where the original Christian message was most relevant to the first —but these are not for the most part points of agreement and conformity, but points of difference and confrontation.

Biblical modernism was busy, a generation ago, reduc-

29

ing these points of confrontation, just as fundamentalism was busy multiplying them—modernism denying that the Bible and the church had anything to say which we did not already know to be true, and fundamentalism affirming that what the Bible and the church had to say was mostly what we knew quite well was not true. Both lacked relevance—modernism because it made Christianity too easy; and fundamentalism, not because it made Christianity too hard, but because it made it hard at the wrong places. The modernist would have reduced the whole essential opposition of the church and the world to the status of mere accidental cultural differences between the first century and the twentieth; the fundamentalist would have elevated all the accidental cultural differences between the first century and the twentieth to the status of essential and permanent differences between the church and the world.

The first century church *does* stand against the modern world; the events of the first century *do* confront and challenge—the harsh biblical term is "scandalize"—the twentieth. This fact any modernism is in danger of forgetting. But the points where they thus challenge the twentieth are precisely and only the points where they also challenged the first; it is this fact which any fundamentalism or dogmatism tends to ignore. Only through faithful and disinterested effort to see Christianity in its original setting and to hear its message as its first hearers heard it—only through a striving for historical truth—can those points of confrontation and therefore of greatest relevance be discerned. True biblical preaching is preaching which has discerned these points of relevance and in doing so has recovered the authentic meaning of the biblical text.

The biblical scholar and the biblical preacher are each subject to a peculiar peril. The scholar's peril is that of a too narrow specialization—that is, a specialization which is so narrow as to defeat its own end. We have heard, probably *ad nauseam*, that an expert is one who "knows more and more about less and less." There is, of course, a certain partial truth in this epigram as there is in most epigrams; but if by "expert" we mean a competent scholar in any field, we must recognize that he must know "more and more" about "more and more," if he is going really to know "more and more" about "less and less"; or, to say the same thing in the equally true other way, if he is really learning "more and more" about "less and less," he is also learning "more and more" about "more and more." For whatever the particular problem on which he is engaged, if it has any significance at all, its ramifications are literally endless and the context in which it can most fruitfully be examined is literally without limit. The biblical scholar so preoccupied with particular technical problems in his research that he supposes he has nothing to learn from the study of contemporary preaching or theology, not to mention modern philosophy, literature, or politics, is not only mistaken but is also cutting himself off from the possibility of the highest achievement in his own field.

The preacher's peculiar peril in this connection is

that of premature impatience with the specialist. Sometimes one forgets that one must have tools for one's work and that it often takes longer to make or acquire the necessary tools than to do the final and more obviously relevant job. I read *Robinson Crusoe* again not long ago and was impressed by how much of his time was spent in making tools, for which as ends in themselves he had no use at all. He spent months making a shovel just as we may spend months learning Greek. Both the shovel and the Greek are, perhaps, more than one step removed from final relevance, but for the achievement of certain ultimately relevant goals, they may be not only relevant but indispensable. Or perhaps our conception of relevance itself is premature, and consequently superficial or too crassly utilitarian. We dismiss the findings of the specialist before we have had time to discover how much they have to contribute to our understanding of matters far beyond the limits of his apparently narrow field. Or we reject, because from our *present* point of view it is irrelevant, what might have given us a new point of view from which whole new ranges of relevance would have been disclosed. We get impatient with our expert guides because they are not *always* presenting us with a splendid view. Or perhaps we decide to dispense with guides entirely, preferring the view we already have or can easily find for ourselves to following the twisting path through the long dark passes till we reach the peak. We reject out of hand because it does not provide us with a sermon what if given time might have provided us with a gospel!

The educational process, the growth toward intellectual maturity, might be described—indeed might almost be defined—as the process of discovering constantly wider areas of relevance. But this process is not painless, nor is its goal at every moment in full view. Certainly one mark of the wise man is his ability to be interested in a surprising number of things, and, as it may seem to others, in surprisingly uninteresting things—and all because he has learned that possibilities of relevance often exist in quite unsuspected and very unpromising places. He has learned that truth of whatever sort if given time has a way of becoming, not only interesting, but important; that every discoverer of truth, in whatever field, has something significant to say, although one must sometimes be willing to wait for the significance to reveal itself; that truth is ultimately one, and that therefore no single bit of it, in any field, can in the last resort be alien or irrelevant.

But if it can be said of all searchers after truth that they are engaged on a common task and are therefore under the obligation of mutual trust and helpfulness, can this not be said with special point of the biblical scholar and the preacher? They belong to, and are servants of, a particular community, and that community is the community of Christ. They are both seeking to understand the meaning of this community—its origins, its nature, and its task. The scholar or the preacher who says to the other, "I have no need of thee," has failed to see, not only the nature of the church and the meaning of membership in it, but also the nature of his own work. Because he is not willing to receive, he cannot truly

33

give. And in failing to contribute to a common achievement, he falls short of any significant achievement of his own. A willingness to learn from others which is both eager and patient is not only one of the graces of charity; it is the very heart of wisdom.

Chapter III

Scholars and Preachers

HAVING LAID DOWN SOME GENERAL PRINCIPLES CON-
cerning the relation of the Bible to preaching, we may
now discuss how these principles can be implemented.
So far we have been concerned with the preacher's use of
Scripture in the large; now we consider his use of
particular texts in particular sermons. Is the preacher's
use limited to the conscious intention of the text? If
not, how far or under what conditions can he depart
from that original meaning? Can the development of
merely implicit meanings be regarded as legitimate? To
what extent can the long use in the church of a biblical
text as having a certain meaning justify its continued
use with that same meaning even though historical
study has made quite clear that the text originally
meant something quite different? Is it legitimate to
focus attention in a sermon on a particular and compara-
tively unimportant aspect of the meaning of a text,
even though one thus presents a highly disproportionate
treatment, in which the main point of the text may
receive scant attention or indeed may not appear at all?
Although I shall not venture to offer detailed or defini-

35

tive answers to these several questions, they indicate the general problem of this chapter. It is by no means a simple or easy problem to solve.

The first step in the solution, however, is clear enough: the preacher's use of the text must *start from* a knowledge of its original sense. Whatever he does with a text, he must *know* what he is doing; and this means knowing what the text really meant to its writer and what the writer intended it to mean to its first readers. Of course, it is impossible to know what some biblical texts were originally intended to convey, whether because the original phrasing is uncertain or ambiguous, or for some other reason. But there is no excuse for failing to know as much as can be known, and in most cases the original meaning is clear enough if one searches for it. Ernest C. Colwell writes:

Generally speaking there are only two methods of interpreting the Bible. They are the "modernizing" and the "historical" methods. Each of these methods has numerous modifications and forms, but these two are separated from each other by a gulf which is so wide that it dwarfs all the minor divisions. The method which has been called the modernizing method has its feet firmly planted in the period in which the interpreter lives; it finds the Bible's basic meaning with reference to the "modern" period, in which the interpreter is naturally most interested. The historical method, on the other hand, finds the Bible's basic meaning with reference to the situation in which the Bible was written.[5]

The stress in the last two sentences should fall on

the word "basic." We have seen that none of us will really understand what the Bible said to its own age who does not also hear it speaking to ours. But there is no doubt, as the preceding chapter will have made clear, where the process of understanding *begins*; it begins with the meaning of the text in its original setting. The *basic* meaning, for the preacher no less than for the biblical scholar, is the historical meaning.

Now we all recognize that the preacher is under extraordinary temptation to neglect this first step. He is not a historian with a concern for history for its own sake. He is concerned with the meaning of the gospel for his own period and he has large responsibilities for modern men and women, in his congregation and in society at large, whose problems and needs demand his attention from every side. He is under the most urgent pressure to "serve the present age." It is not strange that his first question about a biblical text is often, "How can I use this text to help my people?" rather than, "What did this text originally mean?"

The tendency to neglect the original sense is enhanced by a not uncommon view of the nature of the Bible as the Word of God. As such, according to this view, it is not only infallible, but also incalculably weighty and mysteriously pregnant. There is literally no limit to what the text may mean. Whatever the words suggest to the interpreter—or, as he would often say it, whatever the Holy Spirit imparts—must be what, or at least a part of what, the text is intended to convey. Since the meaning the words first had for its readers does not in any degree determine or limit their real

37

meaning, why trouble to inquire into it? Thus it happens that the preacher's own conceptions take precedence to the words of Scripture itself, and the very affirmation of the Bible's unlimited meaning amounts to a denial to it of any definitive meaning at all. Perhaps none of us would express himself quite as the preacher did who said, "I am no mathematician, no biologist, neither grammarian, but when it comes to handling the Bible, I knocks down verbs, breaks up prepositions, and jumps over adjectives"; but not infrequently we act with equal arrogance, riding roughshod over the clearly intended meaning of the text in order to make our own point. It is amazing, when you think about it, that one can do this under the impression that in thus disregarding the original meaning of the words of Scripture one is in some way exalting the Word of God. If the Word of God was spoken in and through a historical event or development, then it becomes vital to recover that development or event as fully and truly as we can. Hence the importance of the biblical scholar's work. Hence also the importance of the preacher's beginning his use of a text with as clear a grasp as possible of its original meaning.

It is not necessary to say much here about method in securing this grasp. The ground has often been gone over and is familiar to us. Obviously, one must know, if possible, what the text actually says—that is, one should know the Greek or Hebrew text. If manuscript or other ancient evidence makes the exact wording uncertain, the preacher should be prepared to consider the various possibilities and to reach an intelligent conclusion as to the text's proper form. He must then translate the text, utilizing the large resources which modern scholarship makes available—lexicons, grammars, concordances, commentaries—to the limit of his abilities (and with practice and discipline these abilities can be increased). If the preacher does not know the original languages, he must depend entirely upon others both for the determination of the correct text and for its translation. But for such a preacher also rich resources are available in the large number of excellent modern translations, a comparison of which should go far toward establishing for him both the most authoritative text and the most accurate English rendering.

One who translates a text, or settles upon a translation made by someone else, has already begun to interpret. Indeed translation can hardly become sure and fixed until the process of interpreting is complete, or at least far advanced. This process of finding out what a text originally meant is often neither simple nor easy. One must know as well as possible the biblical book from which the text is taken—the historical and cultural situation which is reflected in it and to which it is addressed; its general purpose and the general course of its argument; and the relation of the text to this argument and purpose. One must see the text, as far as one can, in its total and in its immediate context. One must seek intelligently to put oneself in the place of the writer and to understand him in the light of what can be known about him—his circumstances, his experiences, his ideas, his responsibilities. One must try to enter imaginatively into the situation of the first readers and to sense as concretely as possible their interests and needs. Again we may remind ourselves that modern biblical scholarship is able richly to help us in gaining this kind of historical understanding.

The learning which the preacher thus acquires does not always need to be retailed to his congregation in his sermon. A biblical sermon is not a lecture on the Bible—whether a humorous lecture as some of Patton's sermons would seem to have been, or a more serious lecture. It is true that sermons ought to be more enlightening as to the Bible itself and the literary and historical problems which it presents than they often are. A preacher interested in raising the general level of his congregation's knowledge of the Bible will find ways of sharing directly with them the more important results of his own studies. And Patton is quite right in saying that people are much more ready to be informed than we often give them credit for being. Still, at least so far as the sermon is concerned, the imparting of mere information will be a subordinate and incidental interest. But that does not mean that the preacher's own possession of the available and relevant literary and historical knowledge as he prepares to preach on a text is in any sense or degree subordinate and incidental. Such knowledge is indispensable. However legitimate or illegitimate may be various ways of using a text in preaching, there can be no proper use of a text which does not *start* in as true an understanding as can be secured of its original or historical sense.

But what may a sermon legitimately *do* with a text?

40

What uses may properly be made of it? What "departures" from it can be allowed? In a word, what answer or answers can be made to the questions with which this chapter began?

Usually, we shall find, if one starts with a clear recognition of the original sense of the text, this kind of problem will not arise. If the text is a vital part of Scripture, and therefore really worth preaching on at all, and if one sees what it really means in its scriptural and historical context, one will ordinarily be moved to preach *that meaning*. One's sermon will be an effort to convey and apply the original sense of the text, and there will be no question of "departing" from it. One's very understanding of the text's original meaning, as we were seeing in the preceding chapter, involves a lively sense of its present relevance; and the whole impulse to use the text in preaching grows out of this understanding. In such cases, a knowledge of what the text said to its generation is a knowledge of what it has to say to ours —and the preacher will be interested in presenting and freshly applying precisely that meaning, and no other. If most of our sermons are not related to their texts in this direct and immediate way, we have good reason to suspect the soundness of our preaching methods.

When we speak of the "original sense" of a passage or of its meaning in its "original context," we should have in mind, not simply its logical relations within the sentence, paragraph, chapter, or book in which it is found, but also something vastly richer and more significant. The "original context" is not a mere form of words, but is the actual life of the ancient religious com-

41

munity in which the text was first heard and treasured. I can imagine, for example, three types of sermon on the familiar Gospel story of Bartimaeus, the blind beggar who cried out, as Jesus passed by, "Jesus, Son of David, have mercy on me!" (Mark 10:46) and whom Jesus healed with a word. One sermon will find in the incident the proof that Jesus was the Messiah—he was called "Son of David" and he demonstrated that he deserved the title by his miraculous act. The purpose of the sermon will be to awaken or confirm the belief that Jesus was in truth the Christ. The second sermon will emphasize the human compassion of Jesus. Jesus is walking by, concerned with other business, when the beggar's cry is heard. He stops, asks what the man wants, and graciously fills his need. The purpose of the sermon will be to encourage a similar sensitiveness, courtesy, and generosity. The first of these two sermons can make the better claim to using the text authentically, but it is in the last resort irrelevant, and therefore, however true it may be, it is not a true sermon. No one can be convinced by an incident in the past that Jesus was the Christ, and an intellectual conviction based on a past fact of this kind would not be significant anyhow. The second sermon could make a better claim perhaps to being relevant; but certainly so shallow a use of the text cannot be authentic. The story was not remembered and finally recorded in the Gospel because this kind of meaning was found in it.

But the third sermon will treat the incident, not as a past event from which we can derive true or useful lessons—whether doctrinal or ethical—but as an event in our own history. We are blind Bartimaeus. Christ calls *to us*, "What do you want me to do for you?" It is we who answer, or would answer, "Master, let me receive my sight." And in the measure of our faith we are brought out of our darkness into his marvelous light. It is obvious that only when the text is understood in some such way is it deeply relevant. But it is just as true that only such an understanding is historically authentic. For that is the kind of meaning the text had from the beginning. It was because it answered thus to the realities of the life of the primitive church that it became a part of its preaching and was later embodied in the Gospel. Such use of the text is not fanciful allegorization. It rests on the only adequate kind of exegesis. For if we do not hear such texts as spoken *to us*, we do not hear them as they were heard in the early church, and therefore we do not hear them in their true and original context.

Incidentally, it may be pointed out that the recognition of the fact that the third sermon is the only true one on the text helps solve the problem with which the historical and literary criticism of the Bible seems sometimes to confront the preacher. Once it is seen that the authentic meaning of the text is the meaning it had— and has—in the context of the church's life, questions about who first spoke or wrote it or about how closely it corresponds with some actual incident or fact become largely irrelevant. The truth of the text depends entirely upon how authentically it sets forth the meaning of the historical event as this was known within the early church

43

and as it is known, or can be known, within the life of the continuing historical community.[6]

But sometimes we shall see, and be moved to preach on, meanings of texts which there is good reason to doubt the original writers intended or the original readers recognized. The question of propriety in such a case is a question of whether the meanings are really implicit in the text or are falsely seen or are frankly imported into it. If the meaning of the sermon is not there—either consciously or implicitly—the use of the text is illegitimate, no matter how cleverly the minister may make the mere words of it serve his needs. Often our violations of this principle of propriety are flagrant and unmistakable. No one would argue, for example, that a sermon on the dimensions of life is, in any sense or degree, implicit in Pharaoh's question of Jacob, "How old are you?" But not infrequently the question of propriety is much harder to answer, and great demands are made upon our powers of honest discrimination. Still, however difficult the application in particular cases, the principle stands. One cannot honestly appear to draw out of a text what is not in it. It is neither right nor prudent to rest a sermon on a text which cannot firmly support it.

One must recognize, however, the reality, and often the rich variety, of merely implicit meanings. The full significance of no really great utterance is consciously apprehended by those who first hear it or even by him who first utters it. The great thinker or poet is always saying more than he is aware of saying, and the great

44

builder is always building more wisely than he knows. The words of the Hebrew prophet or psalmist or of Paul or John or even of Jesus himself (indeed, chiefly him) are often pregnant beyond their knowing and true in ways their hearers did not dream of. Some event or development in modern times will sometimes, not only freshly illustrate or confirm an ancient text, but also disclose wholly new dimensions of meaning within it. Occasionally even some personal experience of one's own will reveal some bearing or application of the text of which the original writer could hardly have been aware.

Similarly, an incident in the biblical narrative may illustrate some universal or timeless truth about God, man, duty, or salvation, of which those who recorded it, not to speak of those who originally witnessed it, did not think at all. When Reinhold Niebuhr sees in Jesus' crucifixion between two thieves an exemplification of the truth that conventional society is likely to treat its criminals and its saints in the same way, he is not misusing his text, although almost certainly he is making a point which neither the watchers of the Crucifixion nor the Gospel writers thought of at all. Still the point is a true one, recurrently illustrated in history and in ordinary life, and supremely set forth in the circumstances of Jesus' death for all who have eyes to see it. It is not imported; it is there. In the same way, one may see in Jesus' answer to Martha when she called on him to rebuke her sister or in his answer to the unnamed man who complained against his brother about an inheritance —one may see in Jesus' reply in both cases a reminder that when we stand before God we stand always as defendants, never as plaintiffs. God does not hear our complaints against others; he says rather, "What about you? Look to yourself!" Such a meaning may or may not have been seen in these incidents by the Gospel writer who recorded them, but it is there.

In other words, a sermon is not "departing" from its text when it finds a fresh meaning in it. An authentic use of a text does not need to be a "wooden" use; an imaginative use is not necessarily fanciful and false. Indeed, if our use of a text is really unimaginative and wooden, it cannot be authentic. No rigid rules of propriety in this realm can be laid down. Intelligence, integrity, good taste can alone be relied on, and they alone suffice—provided always the preacher begins with as clear as possible an understanding of the original sense. Without this understanding, he is without rudder or compass in his use of the Scripture, no matter how intelligent, honest, or sensitive he may be. With it he will find it hard to go too far astray.

Chapter IV

Preaching Is Teaching

WE HAVE SEEN THAT THE WORD "PREACHING" IS DERIVED
from the Latin *praedicatio*, which in turn translates the
Greek *kērugma*, a word meaning in the most general
sense, the proclamation of a fact or an event. It is regularly used in the New Testament in describing the message and (in its verbal form) the activity of the Christian
evangelists, who had the supreme "good news" to tell,
the good news that, in Christ, God had visited and
redeemed his people and that salvation was being freely
offered to all who would repent and put their trust in
him. The preachers were the heralds of the kingdom of
God. They announced the fact of God's gracious deed
in Christ and called upon their hearers for the appropriate response of penitence and faith. They were, as
we have seen, the preachers of *the gospel*.

The word "gospel" is associated in our minds primarily with the books at the beginning of the New
Testament; but that is a derived, not the primary, use of
the term. None of the Gospels was originally called by
that name, nor indeed is the word often used in these

books. Luke makes frequent use of the related verbal form which means to "proclaim good tidings," but the noun "gospel" is not to be found in Luke or John and occurs only eleven times in Mark and Matthew together. It appears twice in Acts, once in I Peter, once in Revelation, and nowhere else in the New Testament except in the Pauline epistles—where it is found some sixty times! Paul, who may be suspected of really coining the word in its Christian sense, certainly was not thinking of a book when he used it. He was thinking of the content of the Christian preaching. We do not know exactly how the term came to designate a book or a canon of books. Perhaps this happened under the influence of the first verse of Mark, "The beginning of the gospel of Jesus Christ," a phrase in the opening sentence becoming the title of the book and thus the title of other books of the same kind. Perhaps it occurred under the influence of Marcion, who was the first to canonize any of our New Testament books and whose scriptures contained among others a document quite similar to our Luke but called by Marcion simply "the gospel" (corresponding doubtless to "the law" in the Jewish canon, which he rejected). In support of this explanation can be cited the fact that when the four Gospels came to be established as canonical, they were called not the "gospels" of Mark, Matthew, Luke, and John, but rather the "gospel" (singular) according to Mark, Matthew, Luke, and John. The singular form suggests the original meaning of the word "gospel"— not a book but a message, which might be differently presented by different writers, but which was itself neces-

48

sarily singular and unique. In the very beginning there were no such documents as our Gospels. The "gospel" of God's saving action in Christ was at first not a story written in a book but a proclamation on the lips of the primitive preachers.

C. H. Dodd begins his little book *The Apostolic Preaching*[7] by calling attention to the distinction in the primitive church between preaching and teaching. Teaching (*didachē*), along with exhortation (*paraklēsis*), was for the most part ethical instruction and appeal addressed to persons already established in the faith. Preaching (*kērugma*) was addressed primarily to non-Christians. It was proclamation, not instruction or exhortation. There can be no doubt about the soundness of this distinction—what has been said about the meaning of the word "preach" will indicate as much. I question, however, whether the distinction between "preaching" and "teaching" was as sharp as Dodd implies and, more particularly, that the functions of the preacher and teacher were ever actually separated in the life of the primitive community.

Students of the primitive church are accustomed to speaking (for example, in discussions of the origins and development of the gospel tradition) of "the early Christian preachers and teachers." Do they mean two classes of persons, or are they referring to two kinds of activity which the same persons might carry on? Whatever they mean, it is highly unlikely that two separate classes of functionaries actually existed and a question may appropriately be raised as to how sharply even the two *functions* were distinguished from each other. One could

49

not proclaim the good news of Christ without attempting at the same time to explain its meaning and to support this meaning with arguments and examples, and without drawing out some of its ethical implications. And one could not, in the manner of the teacher, interpret the meaning of the Christian life itself without reminding one's hearers constantly of the event of Christ. Although the verb "preach" most often has as its object some such term as "the gospel" or "the kingdom of God," Paul can (in Romans 2:21) speak about "preaching against stealing." And although it is apparently true that "teaching" was usually addressed to believers, we read (in Acts 13:12) that the pagan proconsul Sergius Paulus "believed, when he saw what had occurred, for he was astonished at the teaching of the Lord." Indeed, there are many indications that "teaching" was a broad term which might include the proclamation of the facts of the gospel as well as ethical instruction and admonition.

As a matter of fact, the distinction between primitive Christian ministries which is most frequent in the New Testament is not between "teachers" and "preachers," but between "teachers" and "prophets." Paul, in the earliest list of church functions and functionaries we have (I Cor. 12:28), speaks first of "apostles," "prophets," "teachers," in that order. The "apostles" almost certainly are the limited group of authoritative leaders in the whole church—those whom, it was believed, Jesus himself, immediately after his resurrection, had commissioned as his representatives and had sent out to proclaim the gospel and to establish churches. With them were associated other evangelists who served under them or accompanied them on their travels—men like Titus, Timothy, Barnabas, Mark—and these also might on occasion perhaps be called "apostles." But, however defined, "apostles" belonged to the church as a whole, not to the local congregations. The principal *local* ministers are the "prophets" and "teachers." It is obvious that preaching will be one of the most important functions of the apostle—he is *par excellence* the evangelist —but are we to suppose that there were not evangelists also in the local churches? Would the gospel be proclaimed there only when an authorized visiting apostle was present? To ask that question is almost to answer it. Every Christian congregation, set in a vast pagan environment, would be aware of a constant evangelistic opportunity and task. But even more important than this is the fact that the "good news" must be, and can be, continually retold. The event of Christ needs to be declared again and again—in the assembly of the saints as well as to the unbelievers. What Dodd calls the apostolic preaching would take place in every local church day after day, week after week. But we do not hear of "preachers" in this connection. The preaching will have been done by the "prophets" and "teachers." What can we know about these ministers of the early church?

The "prophets" are certainly to be seen against the background of Hebrew prophecy. The prophets clearly appear in Israel as early as the beginning of the monarchy but their origins are much earlier. They were "men of God," identified as such by striking personal endow-

51

ment. Such persons are found in every primitive community. They are particularly subject to trance and ecstasy and are felt to be possessed by the divine mana, the mysterious God. They are "inspired." Some of the earliest prophets were men of unusual intelligence and moral power, such as Samuel and Elijah; some of them were wandering dervishes. Amos, Hosea, Isaiah, Micah, and others like them were also prophets. These men of quite extraordinary personal and intellectual gifts would have been careful to distinguish themselves from the common type: "I am no prophet, nor a prophet's son" (7:14), says Amos. But they had this in common with other prophets—and it is the essential thing—that they regarded themselves (or were regarded) as standing in a close relation with God and as having a direct word from him, and they were extraordinarily able to communicate a sense of the reality and the awesome power of the divine.

It was, we may believe, men and women of this kind who were the prophets of the early church. Some of them were undoubtedly of the primitive dervish type, and some of these were conscious or unconscious frauds. A second-century pagan writer, Lucian, wrote an amusing satire on one of these, a man named Peregrinus who succeeded in exploiting the charity, and the gullibility, of the Christians. The writer of the Didache, an early manual of church order, puts congregations on guard against such persons. His directions for testing the "prophets" are simple but shrewd. If a visiting prophet asks for hospitality, he is to be allowed to stay "not more than one day, or if necessary two; but if he

52

stays for three days, he is a false prophet. . . . No prophet who orders a meal in a spirit shall eat of it; if he does he is a false prophet. . . . If in a spirit he asks for money or anything else, do not listen to him." The writer sums up: "Not everyone who speaks in a spirit is a prophet; he is a prophet only if he has the behavior of the Lord." But there can be no doubt that most of the prophets proved true.

Behavior was not the only test; the true prophet will "teach the truth." His words will edify the church. Paul also makes this point in speaking of the more extreme ecstatics in Corinth, those who speak in tongues. Although it did not occur to him to question the genuineness and value of this kind of ecstatic speaking, he did not give it the name of prophecy. This name he reserved for intelligible speech which proved its worth by edifying the congregation. "One who speaks in a tongue speaks not to men but to God; for no one understands him, but he utters mysteries in the Spirit. On the other hand, he who prophesies speaks to men for their upbuilding and encouragement and consolation." (I Cor. 14:2-3.)

How then did the prophets differ from the teachers? I do not believe that the two classes were altogether distinct from each other in the primitive church or that any clear separation even of function existed between them.[8] The term "teacher" designated the broader, the more general, category. The prophets were all teachers, but not all the teachers were prophets—just as the apostles may all have been prophets, but not all the prophets were apostles. The prophets were teachers with a

53

special kind of inspiration, men and women peculiarly endowed with the mysterious power to communicate the presence of God. The prophet was possessed by the Spirit in a particular way and was capable of "teaching" with special potency, moving the emotions and the conscience as well as enlightening the mind. One is not to suppose that the "teacher" was without these "pneumatic" gifts; he also was inspired "by the same Spirit" (I Cor. 12:4-11). But he was less richly endowed in this respect, although in other ways (as for example in the ability to explain coherently and with rational persuasion) he might, in a particular case, have been more gifted than many of the prophets. Still, just as the prophets with widest and highest authority in the church were the "apostles," so the more inspired teachers were the "prophets." There is nothing to indicate that the several groups had different things to say—all were concerned with the "gospel," the "preaching," and all were concerned with enlightening the minds and consciences of their hearers. All had both evangelistic and pastoral responsibilities. Apostles were teachers as well as preachers, and the local prophets and teachers were all preachers as well as teachers. The apostles and prophets, at least, will also have had other tasks. Thus, the apostles carried important administrative burdens and the prophets were apparently usually responsible for the conduct of the common worship of the congregation. So much for the meaning of these terms in the primitive church.

The modern minister, like the ancient bishop, combines as far as one man can the functions of all three

54

of the primitive types. He is the pastor and administrative head of the church, the leader of worship, and the preacher. Our concern with him is in the last of these capacities, and in that capacity he corresponds most closely with the teacher. If endowed with a certain kind of sensitivity and eloquence, if capable above other teachers of feeling and communicating the concrete reality of the Spirit, he will stand close to the primitive prophet in type (and in the modern situation, as well as in the ancient, there will be many false prophets, for there are many kinds of spirits, now as then). But the preacher, whether he be also a prophet or not, will be a teacher. The word "teaching," however, implies no limited range of content. In the ancient sense it is concerned with nothing less than the proclamation and interpretation of the gospel—the announcement of God's deed in Christ and the opening up of the whole vast wealth of its meaning for human history and for every man. And the criterion of its success is the building up of the church both in numbers and in understanding and devotion.

Not infrequently the terms "teaching ministry" or "teaching sermon" are used among us in a restrictive, if not a slightly disparaging, sense. Preaching is supposed to be something more—or even other—than teaching. The preacher who cannot really "preach" may be said to "teach." We need to realize that unless preaching is teaching, it is not preaching. To be sure, preaching is highly distinctive teaching because of the character and significance of its content, because of its setting in worship, because of the personal relationship

55

which the preacher sustains with his message, and because he is addressing himself, not only to the minds of his hearers, but also to their wills—indeed to them as whole persons. He is seeking, not only to convince them, but also to bring them to a decision. These notes of distinction we shall be considering in subsequent chapters. But the preacher is still basically the teacher. His primary responsibility is for the understanding of the truth and meaning of the gospel and for the communication of this truth and meaning (including all its implications he is given to see) as clearly and persuasively as possible. Unless it is such teaching, it is mere sound, or perhaps sound and fury, however unctuous or stirring it may be. When preaching ceases to be really illuminating, it becomes, not "prophecy" as we sometimes vainly suppose, but "tongues," and "tongues" of a peculiarly irresponsible and meaningless kind. According to Paul the speakers in tongues are speaking to God. Preaching which is unilluminating—whether because it is unintelligible, irrelevant, or trite—speaks neither to God nor to man.

We have defined "teaching" in this connection very broadly, as I am sure we should; but we may appropriately close this discussion with a reminder that even in the narrower sense in which the term is ordinarily used when we speak of "teaching sermons"—even in that sense, teaching is of the greatest importance. We often hear of the "illiteracy" of congregations by and large—men and women intelligent about other things who are utterly naïve or hopelessly confused in their thinking about the church and its faith. Why is this true? No doubt many causes can be found; but will not one of the most significant of them be the failure of the church's preaching to be really educative? Often this failure will appear in the haphazard character of the subjects of the preaching—the preacher making no effort apparently to deal comprehensively over an extended time with the important themes of Christian faith and life, whether by following the liturgical church year or in some other way. But the failure may also manifest itself in the consistently elementary level of the preaching—the same themes being handled in the same way year after year, the preacher apparently having no expectation that his congregation may grow in understanding. There is great wisdom in not giving meat to persons who are ready only for milk; but something is wrong when a congregation is permanently on an all-milk diet.

Must we not confess that what is often wrong in such cases is that the preacher takes only milk himself?

Chapter V

Preaching Is Personal

WE HAVE SEEN THAT ALL PREACHING, WHATEVER ELSE IT is besides, is teaching; but obviously not all teaching— even teaching about a religious subject—is preaching. At one of our seminaries there is an endowed "sermon" delivered each year by a visiting scholar. A few years ago the subject of this sermon was "The Western Text of Acts." Now no fault is being found with the preacher on this particular occasion, which has its own traditional proprieties, and those of us who have worked at problems of textual criticism know how fascinating this subject can be. But can you imagine the pastor of a congregation announcing this theme for his Sunday morning sermon? And yet we sometimes do as badly, "preaching" on the authorship of Hebrews, or the number of Isaiahs, or the organization of the missionary work of our denomination, or the constitution of the United Nations. A sermon is obviously not a lecture. But how is it different? What, besides its generally religious or even Christian content, distinguishes preaching from other types of teaching? The remaining chapters of this book will be concerned with this question. The answer,

I believe, lies in the personal nature of preaching and in the relation in which it stands to common worship, on the one hand, and to the Spirit and the event of Christ, on the other.

We may begin, then, by emphasizing the *personal* character of preaching. The preacher is a person addressing other persons. His speech is directly and immediately to a hearing group and out of personal experience and commitment. Any teacher is addressing a hearing group, of course, but he may be speaking, less as a person, to other persons, than as an expert on the subject of his lecture to an audience presumably interested in learning more about it. The preacher is not an expert in religion informing interested learners, but a person who is sharing some of his most intimate and profound experience with other persons. Preaching is not speech about religion; it is a religious person speaking.

It is this personal character of preaching which makes the moral integrity of the preacher so important. It is often argued that the validity and effectiveness of the sacraments of the church are neither enhanced nor impaired by the moral character of the officiating priest. It would be much harder to make this point about the preaching. How good we are as preachers depends—not altogether, but (make no mistake!) primarily—on how good we are as men. And let there be no misunderstanding about what I mean by "how good we are." I mean how honest we are, how straightforward and sincere, how free from pride, sham, pretentiousness, self-complacency, or preoccupation with our own problems. I mean how penitent we are, with what passion of desire we are seeking God, how ready we are to submit to his will, how concerned we are to please him, how constantly aware we are of our need of his forgiveness, how faithfully dependent upon his grace, how unyielding in our discipline, how unwithholding in our devotion. I mean how genuinely concerned we are about others, how eager to understand them and to help, how patient with them and how loving, and how sensitive to their deeper wants because we are living truly and deeply ourselves. None of us will be willing to claim that we are in this sense good men; but we will have known such men and we will all know that such goodness is a more important qualification of the preacher than any amount of either learning or eloquence.

Learning and eloquence, indeed, may like riches be a snare to trap us and destroy our souls. It is as hard for the so-called big preacher to enter the kingdom of heaven as for any other successful man or woman— probably harder. The temptations to pride are almost irresistible, and since the preacher is in a position where he must appear humble in order to have socially acceptable grounds for his pride, the even grosser sin of hypocrisy is all but inescapable. To the man of many talents, as well as to the man of great wealth, Jesus says, "If you would have life, give up all reliance upon your possessions, renounce all your pride in them and in the power they give you; come, take up your cross and follow me," and the one as often as the other "must go away sorrowful," for wealth is not our only possession, or our most intimate, or that in which we may take the greatest pride. Besides, one can solve—or at least escape from—the problem of wealth by getting rid of it; but one cannot give away one's talents. It is a sin to flaunt them or selfishly to exploit them, but it is equally a sin to bury them.

And, of course, the one-talent man can be as proud of his one talent as the ten-talent man of his ten, and quite as selfish in the use he makes of it. The wealthy man may be in peculiar danger of covetousness but the poor are not exempt. Occasionally the rich man does not merely cast in out of his abundance, but actually consecrates the abundance itself, and sometimes, far from giving away all her living, the poor widow grasps both her mites. It may be true that "all power corrupts," but one does not need to possess power in order to be corrupted by it; one needs only to be ambitious for it, to envy others the possession of it. Covetousness, mean ambition, jealousy, and pride can twist and destroy the soul of the man with few gifts as of the man with many. There is no true and honest preacher who does not often feel with Paul the desperate fear, "lest after preaching to others" he himself "should be a castaway." This is a healthy and very realistic fear, especially as we grow older and the muscles of our discipline tend to slacken and the pulses of our devotion tend to beat more slowly. Is it not strange, when one looks at it in a certain way, that the less prospect we have of enjoying this world in any case, the more precious it is likely to become for us? It seems easier for youth to give up everything than for age to surrender the little it has left. This is as true for ministers as for others. Demas is not the last minister who forsook his calling "having loved this present world." This "forsaking" does not need to be overt, and usually is not. Most Demases keep on going through the offices of their profession, and probably for the most part do not themselves know how far away from Christ they have fallen and how cold and dead have become the once flaming coals upon the altar of their hearts.

Like everyone else connected with theological education, I often have to deal with a student struggling against what appears to be a call to the ministry. One of the most frequent of his pleas is, "I am not good enough to be a minister." The invariable answer to this plea is: "But nobody is or can be. Indeed, the person who most clearly and certainly is unfitted for the ministry would be the one who thought himself good enough for it." This is obviously and altogether true, of course; and yet the student's instinctive feeling of a special connection between spiritual goodness and the work of the minister is sound. The medical student is certainly much less likely to say, "I am not a good enough man to be a doctor"; or the law student, "I am morally unworthy of being a lawyer." It would be hard indeed— and intolerably presumptuous—to set up anything like an adequate moral test for the candidate for the ministry, for the kind of goodness we are talking about cannot be measured in legal terms. But there are character tests which the minister must meet—in the secret places of his own heart, if nowhere else—and the true success of his ministry rests, first of all, on his meeting them.

Whenever I think of the men in the ministry who

have helped me most, I think not of the gifted but of
the good. Some of the good were also gifted, but as I
think about them, that is a quite incidental fact.
Whether I knew them recently or years ago, I remember
principally what they were, not what they said. In the
pulpit, as well as outside it, what they really gave me
was themselves.

This essentially personal character of preaching bears
also in an important way upon the preacher's preparation to preach. The answer to the vexing problem
whether it is better to write out one's sermons or to
speak extemporaneously lies at this point. Which method
a particular preacher adopts does not really matter so
long as the nature of preaching as personal communication is not violated, that is, so long as the sense of personal contact between preacher and hearers is main-
tained on both sides. The successful preacher who writes
out his sermons is able imaginatively to place himself
as he writes in the presence of his congregation and in
the situation of the service of worship and thus to put
into his manuscript what he will actually feel moved to
say when the moment of speaking comes. But the formal sermon, whether written or not, may actually
separate the preacher from his congregation, becoming
a barrier to communication rather than a means of it.
Have you not often felt, as you listened to a preacher:
"If he would only throw away that sermon and really
talk to us, things might begin to happen!"

We are dealing here with what is perhaps the supremely difficult, and the supremely important, prob-

lem in the art or technique of preaching—namely, the problem of how to make the necessary preparation without losing the reality of personal communication. Now there will be no dispute about the necessity of preparation—and moreover that one's preparation must include not merely reading and reflection of a generally helpful kind (although this kind of preparation for preaching is important and is often neglected), but also the composition in some detail of what one wants to say on each particular occasion. Indeed, would we not have to confess that one of the reasons our preaching is not more effective is that we do not habitually give enough—and serious enough—attention to preparing our sermons. We will all recognize that this is not the deepest cause of failure and that it would not be a cause at all if there were not deeper ones. I mean to say that if we were right as regards the substance of our preaching, we would not need to be greatly troubled about the form and style of it. We might not speak according to the most approved models of homiletical art, but we would speak effectively enough. Paul tells us that he did not know much about the rules of oratory and that many regarded him as a shoddy speaker; but who can doubt that Paul was an effective preacher of the gospel? Still, though Paul may not have been a master of style, there can be no doubt whatever that he spent a great deal of hard thought on what he would say in his preaching, and that he often gave serious attention to how he would say it. Certainly all of this is true if he bestowed the same care on his sermons as on his letters.

The truth of the matter is that we can easily distinguish too sharply between substance and style, whether in preaching or in any other analogous realm. Capacity to think and feel and ability to express go along together much more closely than we often suppose. Certainly this is true of our thinking. We think in words. One who cannot write or speak a clear sentence does not have a clear thought. The course in English composition which I remember best had as its text a book called *Sentences and Thinking*.[9] The book was good. The *title* was perfect! As for our *feelings*, it is true that they may well run too deep for tears, much less for words. But when we are thus inarticulate, let us be sure that it is because our feelings are so deep and not because our speech is so meager, lazy, and unschooled. After all, the great poets manage to express some of their deeper feelings. And though one must believe that even they can say only a part of what they feel, one suspects that they can feel so much partly because they can say so much. Mastery of the technique of expression and capacity for insight and true emotion go along together in any art; and so related are they as cause and effect that it is often impossible to say with which the circle begins. The preacher, then, who struggles to acquire an adequate style, whether by writing or rewriting in his study or by saying and resaying his sentences and paragraphs to the woods or the sea (as we are told Demosthenes did), is doing more than polishing the surface of his preaching; the whole substance of it is in some degree involved.

We have all had to bear the preacher who does not

prepare to preach. He may be the preacher of some "primitive" sect who follows very literally the injunction of the Gospel that one must not take thought in advance of what one will say and who depends completely on the promise that the Spirit will give both the message and the appropriate words when the time comes. Or he may be the much less admirable—and unfortunately less rare—preacher who relies only on a certain glibness which he has by nature or has acquired. But whether of one sort or the other, we know how unedifying the discourse of an unprepared preacher is, especially if he must speak Sunday after Sunday to the same people. I recall my father's telling about a preacher of his acquaintance who boasted that he never prepared a sermon but that when the moment for speaking came it was as though a great funnel were placed on the top of his head and the Lord poured out the words he was to speak. My father went on to say that having later heard this preacher, he decided that the funnel must have been placed upside down with the little end up. Many a preacher much too sophisticated to believe in the funnel actually follows the same line and is equally irresponsible and ineffectual.

And yet almost as bad as the lack of preparation is the preparation which calls attention to itself. The sermon must not appear as something skillfully contrived, so that the attention of the hearer is being constantly drawn away from what is being said to the clever, or perhaps beautiful, way in which the preacher is saying it. As a matter of fact, the sermon as such will ideally not appear at all. The purpose and real nature of preaching are as certainly defeated and violated by the sermon which calls attention to itself by its skillfulness as by the sermon which calls attention to itself by its sloppiness. The sermon will be there, of course; but the less conspicuous it is, the better. The essential elements in the preaching situation on the human side are the preacher and the congregation; the sermon is not a third element, but the action of one of the elements on the other, or, better perhaps, the movement of one of the elements toward the other. If the sermon as a distinct element comes into view, so that the preacher is thinking not about the congregation and what he wants to say to them, but about the sermon he prepared last week, the words of which lie before him in a manuscript or have been memorized, and if the congregation has the impression that it is hearing, not the preacher but this same sermon—in such a situation authentic preaching is not taking place. A sermon is not a literary essay; it is an act of oral communication. And yet it must be carefully prepared, planned not alone in its general outline but as regards its very language. Must it not be agreed then that the central problem in the technique of preaching is how to make such preparation without impairing the direct and personal character of preaching itself?

I have no solution to propose. It is likely indeed that the problem must be solved by each preacher for himself, and that no two solutions will be precisely the same. But the aim of the preparation is clear; it is a man prepared, not a sermon prepared. The sermon must be an element in the man's own personal readiness for the occasion of preaching. The sermon must not be thought of as doing the preacher's job for him, or even of being the mere instrument with which he does it. The sermon at its truest and best is the man himself doing his work. The sermon is the preacher preaching—an action, not a thing. It is an act of personal expression and communication, not a deposit of previous experience and reflection. It is this fact that makes it so difficult to preach an old sermon. The sermon is an intimate personal creation belonging essentially to the moment of preaching itself. The anticipation of the moment must completely dominate the mood in which the preacher prepares to preach. The more truly, creatively, and vividly he can anticipate that moment, the more intensely he can experience it in advance, the more appropriate and effective his preparation can be. He will be preparing, not a sermon, but himself; or to say it perhaps better, his preparation of a sermon will actually be a preparation of himself and his preparation of himself will be in part the preparation of a sermon.

The sermon then is an expression of the man. It is not an airing of the preacher's opinion, even opinions about important matters, but a sharing of his most intimate and serious convictions. It is more than that; he dares to believe—indeed he cannot help believing—that what he declares has come to him, even to him, as the Word of God. He is thus burdened by a unique sense of responsibility and uplifted by a unique sense of privilege. "The Lord hath spoken, who can but prophesy?" (Amos 3:8 K.J.V.) "Woe is unto me, if I preach not." (I Cor. 9:16 K.J.V.) In some ways the artist stands in the same relation to his work. Think of Ghiberti and the doors of the Florentine baptistery on which he labored fifty years. The great doors were not so much his work as his life. The preacher's work is personal in the same intimate and essential way. He has been given something—he, uniquely and personally—which he must try to declare. He has been admitted to "the secret place of the tabernacle of the Most High" and knows that he has heard there a word which, in its concreteness and particularity, no one else has heard. Of this peculiar sense of vocation he will not speak often, or at all. (Note how loath Paul is to speak of it in II Cor. 12.) It is too significant, too sacred, and too intimately his own. But he carries the joy, and the burden, of it in his heart, and it gives meaning not only to his preaching ministry as a whole, but to every occasion of preaching.

But preaching is personal, not only because it arises out of this deeply personal sense of vocation and because √ when it is really taking place the preacher is a real person seeking to express what is to him as a person most important and most profoundly true, but also because it is addressed to persons. In a way this goes without saying, for the very word "person" implies intercourse with other persons. To speak to others as a person is by definition to speak to them as persons. For a while I was the chaplain of an educational institution where we had many visiting preachers; it was noteworthy how often the preacher seemed to be under the impression that at a university people were students, not persons, the sermon turning out to be a lecture on religion, or something else, rather than a proclaiming of the judgment and love of God and a call to penitence and obedience. In other words, the preacher was prevented from speaking as a person, and therefore, it may be, helpfully and creatively, by his false assumption that we were not prepared to listen as persons.

This does not mean that what is said helpfully to some may with equal helpfulness be said to all. It is quite possible that the good sermon the visiting preacher had given to his own congregation the week before might not have been appropriate in the college chapel, although it is much more likely that it would have been. Still, the language and form, and to some extent the substance, of genuine personal communication will differ on different occasions. What reaches the very hearts of one group may be simply unintelligible to another. What speaks decisively to the felt needs of some may only confuse others. Conversely, what is very relevant and useful to one congregation may be too obvious to be interesting or really helpful to another. It should be said in this connection, however, that what is spoken from the heart, simply, directly, and honestly, will probably reach other hearts. Humble and simple people can grasp truths as profound as any scholar, provided they are truths known concretely in experience rather than mere abstractions—and these are the only truths properly belonging to preaching anyhow. On the other hand, directness, simplicity, and sincerity will certainly not offend the more enlightened. For being simple does not mean necessarily being superficial or obvious. And a congregation, however well educated or sophisticated, will be better served, whether it knows it or not (and it probably will know it), by the honest but relatively ungifted preacher, who knows and speaks to the profound personal needs of his hearers, than by the brilliant practitioner of a mere art, however clever he may be or however skillfully constructed and impeccable may be the essay he delivers as a sermon on Sunday morning.

What we are doing here is simply repeating the fact that preaching must be relevant, with the qualification that by "relevance" in this connection we mean relevance to the personal life of one's hearers. Preaching is addressed to individuals and must be aimed at meeting their personal needs. These individuals are, of course, members of communities—of church, of nation, of family, and the like. One cannot speak to them without taking into account the context of group or corporate existence in which they are involved. But one must speak to *them*. The wider context is of concern only as it affects *them*. The individual hearer, in his own personal situation, is the necessary focus of the preacher's attention.

He must be acquainted, to be sure, with contemporary literature, with contemporary scientific developments, with contemporary theological and philosophical thought. He must understand, as far as possible, the spirit of his times. But this is true only because his people are personally and individually affected by these factors. Quotations from literature, allusions to technology, even theological discussions are irrelevant, and therefore worse than useless, unless they illuminate the personal situation of the hearer, helping him to understand him-

71

self better, to see his duty more clearly, to know more truly the meaning of the gospel, actually to grasp the help God offers in Christ. "Learned" sermons can be as bad as clever ones.

In the same way, the relevance of discussions of current events and of current political and economic issues is determined in every part by their bearing on the personal life of the members of the congregation. Thirty years ago or so, when I was in seminary, we were constantly hearing that the preacher ought to be a prophet —a prophet, not in the sense of that term we were considering in the preceding chapter, but in a quite different sense. The "prophet" was a preacher whose sermons were almost entirely descriptions and denunciations of social evils—war, inequity in industry, racial discrimination, and the like. These "prophetic" fulminations of the preacher were usually directed, not only at the evils, but also at his congregation—as though these men and women were any more responsible for them than he was! Usually, too, he had nothing to propose, whether as a solution of large-scale evil or as a way of life for the individual in the presence of it. And when, for all their patience, the people became tired of coming to church to be fed, and instead of bread receiving stones (even the stones thrown at them!) and decided they wanted another preacher, the "prophet" was sure he was a martyr for the truth, a victim of economic and political reaction. Actually, much more often than not, he suffered because he failed to speak as a person to other persons, failed to deal with people where they were in terms of their own (to use a current phrase) existential situation, that is, failed really to preach.

Needless to say, one cannot thus preach, without taking into account the economic and political facts which condition men's lives and the economic and political issues they confront. There is a judgment of God against the unjust orders of this world as certainly as against the sins of individuals, and we must seek a new and better society, not simply regenerated persons. But the discussion of social issues (or anything else, for that matter) is appropriate and helpful in preaching only as it illuminates the situation, including the duty, of the individual hearer. For every preacher of the social gospel who is rejected by his congregation, another can be found just as much concerned for social justice and just as forthright in expressing his concern in deed and word whose congregation continues to be loyal to him. The difference lies—not always, by any means, but often—in the fact that in one case social evils and objectives are dealt with in the true personal context of preaching whereas in the other it is not so.

We must not forget, on peril of losing our souls, that it is easy to rationalize here and to suppose we are being true to our calling when we are actually being both dishonest and cowardly. Martyrdom, which is always to be deplored (even when it is one's own!), sometimes cannot be avoided. The Christian life is not an escape from social responsibility; the gospel is not an opiate. The preacher who is not sensitive to social injustice, to the plight of the underprivileged, to every instance of man's inhumanity to man, and who does not deal realistically with these conditions in his preaching is not a true preacher. His preaching is not really relevant, however popular it may be for a time. But "realism" in this connection designates a kind of understanding not only of the conditions one is describing, but also of the persons one is addressing, and for one's discussion to be relevant it must be relevant to *them*.

In this connection, as in every other, preaching is personal.

Chapter VI

Preaching Is Worship

WE ARE NOT TURNING FROM THE PERSONAL CHARACTER of preaching but are giving that character a new emphasis and an even more distinctive significance when we recognize the close and necessary connection between preaching and worship. Here is a second distinction between preaching and other kinds of religious teaching. The prophets and teachers in the early church were the leaders of its worship, and this is just as true in the modern church. Moreover, from the beginning also a service of worship has ordinarily provided the situation in which the preacher has spoken. Sometimes, to be sure, the service of worship has been subordinated to the sermon, the whole to the part, and has been thought of as merely a setting for the preacher's discourse. Hymns, confessions, even prayers, have been conceived of as merely preparing the way for the sermon; and the sense of the reality and importance of common worship has been lost. All of this is to be deplored, as much in the interest of true preaching as for any number of other reasons. But, even so, it is still true that the service of worship— not always but often—needs the sermon just as truly as the sermon needs the service of worship. They interpret each other. Each is more significant because the other is present.

But this is not the truest way to describe the connection between preaching and worship. The relationship is more intimate and profound. Unless we conceive of preaching as being itself an act of worship, we miss what is most essential in it and what distinguishes it most radically from other kinds of teaching, religious or secular. The real truth of the matter is not that preaching merely happens usually to be set in a context of worship or that it is most effective when it has that kind of setting. Rather, it cannot be really preaching except in that context. If the context of worship is not there already, the true sermon creates it. Either preaching contributes to, provides a medium of, worship, or it is not preaching at all.

This character of preaching manifests itself in the period of preparation. The sermon is an offering to God—or rather it is the preacher offering himself to God—and the preparation is a disciplined act of devotion. To preach is really to pray with others, to lead others in prayer; to prepare to preach is, certainly under one important aspect, to pray for others and for oneself for the sake of others. I wonder if the private devotional life of most preachers is not largely associated with their preaching and their preparation for it. Certainly one would expect it to be so. It is as the preacher confronts the opportunity of preaching that he will feel most acutely his weakness, his emptiness, his sin. It is then

76

that he will find himself praying with deepest desire: "Oh send out thy light and thy truth; let them lead me . . . to thy holy hill" (Ps. 43:3). And it will be in the course of his work of preparation that he will be most moved to adoration, to gratitude, and to praise.

The recognition that the preparation to preach is the preparation of an offering to God will put in true perspective the importance of that preparation. One does not merely manifest a certain contempt for one's hearers when one comes into the pulpit unprepared; one is guilty of the grossest irreverence toward God himself. We read in the Old Testament about the meticulous way in which the sacrifices and the priests must be made ready for the temple services. How carefully both must be chosen and prepared! We are aware of our freedom from such regulations; the whole system of animal sacrifices has been abolished in Christ, who as the great high priest offered his own blood. But is God less holy than of old, or are we more worthy to approach him? Is not the public worship of the congregation as sacred, as momentous, an event as it ever was? The preacher is priest, as well as prophet and teacher. He has an offering to bring. This offering is not an animal; it is, first of all, himself. He presents himself as "a living sacrifice." His offering, like the lamb on the altar, must be "holy and acceptable." Can it then be impromptu and casual? "Worship," we say, has become more "spiritual." But is it to be taken any less seriously on that account? And yet some of us are habitually unprepared to preach. I have even heard preachers jest about their lack of preparation, and I have already referred to the preacher who

77

boasts of his ability to get along without it. How can we be so grossly presumptuous? How can we dare so much! The unprepared preacher is an unfaithful priest. And unless the preparation of the preacher has begun, continued, and ended in prayer and praise, he is not prepared, no matter how learned, or "beautiful," or clever his sermon, and no matter how long and faithfully he has labored on it.

We think of worship as involving various moods or movements—adoration and thanksgiving, confrontation with God's will, confession of sin, the seeking of forgiveness and of other help we need, affirmation of faith, consecration of life. Preaching participates in every one of these actions. I do not mean, of course, that every sermon will involve them all in equal measure or with equal explicitness, or that they will be involved in preaching in any regular order, as they may be in a liturgy. But preaching will always at least imply all of them, and from time to time one or more of them will constitute the whole intention and effect of the sermon. Surely we can hardly imagine a true sermon which does not convey, very concretely, a sense of the reality, the majesty, the mystery of God and the recognition of our dependence upon him, and which does not move those who hear to adore and praise him for his sovereign goodness. Similarly it can scarcely be true preaching which does not confront men with the law of God in Christ and lead them to repentance and the confession of sin and to renewed obedience. And the basic nature of preaching as the proclamation of the gospel makes it an affirmation of faith—which is why studies of the apostolic preaching and of the earliest creeds always run together.

Now it is of the greatest importance to recognize that the faith and the need of which preaching is a confession are a common faith and need. In the confession of sin the preacher is confessing his own sin as well as that of the congregation, and in the confession of faith the preacher is confessing the faith of the congregation as well as his own. At both points he stands, not above, but within the community and shares completely with it. Some emphasis is appropriate at each of these points for they are frequently disregarded.

We note first, then, that the faith out of which the preacher speaks and which he declares is a common faith. The Christian preacher is not a "free lance." He is a spokesman for the Christian community and stands in a position of great responsibility toward its tradition. His authority is the authority of the truth as it is known, not merely in his own experience but in the experience of the church. He is at best a mere actor, and no preacher at all, unless he is declaring his own personal convictions; but he is not a Christian preacher unless his personal convictions are the convictions of a Christian. The convictions of a Christian, morever, are not simply whatever convictions particular sincere persons of good will, who are also members of the church, may happen to hold but are those of a historical community. The Christian message is not just any kind of message which the individual preacher, however devout and sincere, may have come to accept. It is a message with which the preacher has been entrusted and which he must faithfully transmit unimpaired to others. It is a confession of the church's faith.

Now this faith cannot be rigidly formulated. What was said in an earlier chapter about the *relevance* of biblical preaching needs to be recalled here. One can destroy an ancient faith by insisting on preserving it unchanged in a new time as certainly as by attempting a complete reconstruction of it. The faith of the church, like the church itself, is a living thing. We cannot reconstruct it without destroying it; but, on the other hand, we must not fail to let it grow. We cannot hedge it in. The preacher who merely repeats ancient affirmations with no fresh awareness of their truth for him and his generation is as unfruitful, and as unfaithful to the gospel, as is the preacher who thinks of the ancient terms, if he uses them at all, as a merely convenient means of exploiting his own private notions or of meeting the expectations of the people who come to hear him. But both are obviously wrong. Preaching is a personal, living, confession of the ancient faith of the church.

Or, to say the same thing somewhat differently, preaching is an interpretation, from the inside, of the life of the church—the sort of thing which leads the believing hearer, who shares in the Spirit but may lack the preacher's gifts of discernment and expression, to say "Amen." This "Amen" means: "You have said what I know to be true, although perhaps I could not have said it. You have pointed to realities in my own experience as a participant in the life of the church. You are speaking to me, but more profoundly *for me*. You are confessing *my* faith." The preacher, no less truly than the gospel, must not be hedged in; he must be free to present the meaning of the gospel as that meaning has come home to him. But unless his preaching elicits some such response in the church because it is itself a response to realities in the church's life and a proclamation of the event which gave rise to it and determined its character—unless this is true, his preaching has ceased to be authentic Christian preaching. And we ought not to be surprised if his congregation either rebels or dies.

But if the preacher must confess the church's faith, not simply his own, so he must confess his own sins, not simply the congregation's. The preacher stands as much in need of forgiveness as any hearer. This is a commonplace, of course, and in the prayers in which he leads the congregation this fact is usually fully acknowledged. But the *sermon* sometimes fails to reveal this awareness. The preacher speaks, not as though he were listening for, and to, the Word of God, but as though he were actually God speaking. His manner suggests that he is telling people from some ethical eminence what they are to do. Some years ago Reinhold Niebuhr published an article on "Moralistic Preaching," defined as "holding up high ideals of brotherhood and love to men and nations on the supposition that nothing more than their continued reiteration will ultimately effect their realization." [10] Such preaching consists chiefly of exhortations that we practice the Christian virtues and in vague pictures of how perfect everything would be if we did. The "moralistic" preacher apparently believes that God's ethical demands are thoroughly practicable standards—hardly difficult, certainly not impossible. They could be fulfilled if only we would put forth a little more effort. His preaching consists of talk about love without any sign of awareness either of the impossibility of our doing what love plainly requires in some situations or of the impossibility of our knowing what it requires in others. The conclusion of each sermon is: "I have told you what to do. Now do it!"

It is hardly necessary to point out the falseness, the tediousness, and the futility of this kind of preaching; and the prevalence of it would seem to be indicated by the very connotation which the word "preach" has acquired in our common speech. Parents are told not to "preach" to their children. The most devastating possible criticism of a novel or play is to say that it "preaches." This ill repute of an important Christian word, which basically means the announcement of the supreme good news, may perhaps be blamed partly on the spirit of our age which, if I may be permitted to "preach" a bit, is more impatient of moral authority than it ought to be. But can we deny that it also reflects failures in preaching itself? It is interesting to note that whereas Webster is still able to define the two words "preach" and "preacher" without disparagement, every one of the several terms derived from them is in some degree a term of contempt: preachify, preachment, preachy, preachily, preachiness, preachman, and preacherize. It is doubtless too late to drive such words out of the dictionary, or even to reclaim entirely the basic verb and noun; but those of us who preach may appropriately ask how far the fault lies in others—in their lack of seriousness or sensitivity or even in their perverseness perhaps—and how far it lies in us. And when we do, we are bound to recognize that a part of the answer undoubtedly lies in the easy, shallow "moralism" of much of our preaching.

But preaching can be of this kind only so long at it is not confessional. The preacher who has actually tried to fulfill the law of Christ and who speaks out of his experience will know too well the reality and power of sin in human life as well as the limitations implicit in our finitude. Actually, if he has anything true or helpful to say about the duty of others, it is because he has himself been confronted and confounded by the awful dimensions of his own duty. Such a one sees himself and his hearers as standing on absolutely common ground— under a moral requirement utterly beyond the power of any of them to fulfill and in need of forgiveness, guidance, and help beyond the power of any of them to supply. Effective ethical preaching, like effective doctrinal preaching, is confessional preaching.

Some years ago I heard in a single hour two sermons by two theological students on the Christian ethic of love. The first was a conventional appeal that the congregation and men generally, individually and collectively, follow the way of love. It was pointed out that if we would only do so, mankind would be extricated from all its difficulties. The other preacher, with essentially the same theme, presented in very realistic and personal terms what the following of the way of love would involve in such a world as this. One could sense all the way through his sermon his own earnest but ultimate-

83

ly unsuccessful effort either to escape from the demands of this love or to fulfill them; and in speaking from his own experience, he deeply probed our hearts.

This confessional attitude will also determine one's way of proclaiming the "social gospel." I have referred earlier to the so-called prophetic denunciations of social evils delivered by the preacher quite in the manner of one who thought his congregation was principally responsible for them. Such futile fulminations would be forestalled if the preacher recognized, not only his own involvement in social evil, but also the inevitability of that involvement, equally for himself and others. We are all implicated in the massive inequities and inhumanities of social, political, and economic life—not without guilt and yet not wholly guilty, and in any case utterly unable to extricate ourselves. It is important that we and our congregations be aware of these large-scale social injustices and maladjustments and be sensitive to the enormous human suffering and loss which they entail. It is important that we recognize not only our own implication in them but also our responsibility for the mitigation of them in every possible way. For even when the massiveness and recalcitrance of social evil and our own limitations both in goodness and wisdom are fully granted, still it must be recognized that we could do far more than we do. It is absolutely essential that we see and confess our duty and our sin in this dimension— that we repent not only of our individual sins but of the grosser ones no less our own because we share in them with others. But the preacher can lead us to do

84

this only if he is also repentent—and not merely in-
dignant! In other words, the social problem can be appropriately and fruitfully discussed in preaching only in
a mood of common worship. Our society is sick and
guilty; we all share in this sickness and guilt; we cannot
heal ourselves; only God can forgive us and renew our
life.

It is not unusual for the sermon to be preceded and
followed by prayers. That is not enough: the sermon
must be a prayer itself. True preaching is very close to
praying, the work of the prophet to the work of the
priest.

Chapter VII

Preaching Is Sacrament

IN THE PRECEDING CHAPTER WE WERE CONSIDERING
preaching as an offering to God. The preacher is a priest
representing and speaking for his people, confessing
both their faith and their sin. But true preaching is also
God's gift to us. It is even more than that; it is God
actually giving himself to us. Paul recognizes both
prophecy and teaching as gifts of the Spirit, and the
writer to the Ephesians can speak of apostles, prophets,
evangelists, pastors, and teachers as being themselves
God's "gifts" to the church. Thus, the words of the
preacher are mediatorial in the full sense, not only
gathering up and lifting to God the needs of the congregation, but also becoming a medium of God's communication with us and indeed of his saving action.

The understanding of preaching as an action of the
Spirit is frequently expressed in the New Testament.
Mark records that Jesus' disciples were told in connection with their defense of the gospel before "governors
and kings": "Do not be anxious beforehand what you
are to say; but say whatever is given you in that hour,

for it is not you who speak, but the Holy Spirit" (13:11). This injunction is found in virtually the same words in Matthew (10:19). Luke writes somewhat differently but to the same effect: "Settle it therefore in your minds, not to meditate beforehand how to answer; for I will give you a mouth and wisdom, which none of your adversaries will be able to withstand or contradict" (21:14-15). And later, in Acts (2:4), the same writer describes the disciples as speaking "as the Spirit gave them utterance." He is referring, to be sure, to the miracle of tongues, but he would have said the same thing of prophecy in general, and in fact often does so in effect. Paul, besides consistently representing all Christian preaching as a spiritual gift, can speak of his own preaching as being "in words not taught by human wisdom but taught by the Spirit" (I Cor. 2:13).

Reference has already been made to the modern preacher who, taking literally the injunction of the Gospel, refuses to make any special preparation for preaching but relies upon the Spirit to provide the appropriate words. And we have seen that his hearers are much more likely to be struck by what he lacks than by what the Spirit provides. Whatever truth and importance the Gospel injunction had in its original context, it is obviously not a practicable rule for a responsible teacher of the congregation to follow. The original context, according to all three Gospels, had to do with a hearing before a magistrate where a Christian is required to make his defense. In such a situation it was perhaps the experience of the early church that a very personal and spontaneous explanation, obviously unprepared and unrehearsed, was more effective, because more unmistakably sincere, than any carefully constructed argument was likely to be. This is understandable; indeed, what preacher has not occasionally found himself in situations where the address he had prepared himself to give is, quite clearly, entirely out of place and where he must simply forget what he had so carefully planned, and speak, as we say, out of his heart, following freely where the Spirit leads? But if there are occasional preaching situations of this kind, we know that there is a considerably larger number in which, if we have not "meditated beforehand," we find ourselves with nothing either useful or appropriate to say.

This does not mean that occasionally the preacher should depend on the Spirit, and more often on himself. Far from it; the Spirit must always "give us utterance" if our speaking is to be genuine preaching. Preaching must always be "out of the heart"—that is (paradoxically enough), it must always be not our own deliberate utterance at all, but a response to the Spirit's prompting. Occasionally perhaps the prompting and the response are sudden and momentary. All at once, one hears and must speak. Such ecstatic moments come to most of us—although it must be recognized that they rarely coincide with the formal occasions of preaching. More generally, however, the prompting is less dramatic and irresistible, but mercifully recurrent or persistent; and one's response, although still a true response (and not anything one initiates), is more gradually made. The Spirit *stands* at the door and knocks—knocks quietly but constantly or again and again. One does not finally or fully hear without deliberately listening. The preparation to preach is this action of listening, of trying to hear. Most good sermons are in process of creation for months, perhaps years. At first one is not sure one has heard anything. Gradually one becomes more certain. Finally the knocking demands our full attention, and we know that the time for responding to it has now arrived. The door must be opened. The sermon on the indicated text or theme must be preached. The preacher devotes a solid week perhaps to listening to what the Spirit is seeking to convey. The sermon is his response— no less certainly an authentic *response* because time has been required for making it. Creation indeed in any field is never a sudden thing, although sometimes it appears to be. We may seem to hear suddenly, but we hear only if we have been listening and we would not have begun to listen if we had not already begun to hear. True preaching from start to finish is the work of the Spirit. It is God seeking us, and finding us.

But preaching is this action of God not only in the general way I have been trying to describe—the way in which all creative work is God's action—but also in a more specifically Christian sense. It is essentially and vitally related to the Christian community and to the event in which the community had its rise. To say, as we have been saying, that it is a response to, and therefore in a very real sense a creation of, the Spirit, is virtually to affirm this connection, because "the Spirit" in the Christian sense is that Spirit in whose coming the ancient event essentially consisted and in whose con-

tinuing presence the life of the church essentially consists. Although this relationship of preaching to both
community and event has been often alluded to in the
course of these chapters, it is appropriate to conclude
our discussion by considering it briefly again—and with
special reference to the nature of preaching as the work
of the Spirit, as the revealing act of God.

First, then, we should recognize that when we say
that preaching is prompted by the Spirit we mean that
the prompting comes out of the life of the community.
To be sure it comes from God—but it comes from God
as he is concretely known in the church. To say that the
message of the preacher is given to him by the Spirit is
equivalent to saying it is given him as sharer in the divine
common life which constitutes the essential nature of
the Christian church. It is a striking fact that the first
recorded Christian sermon, that of Peter at Pentecost,
was occasioned by the necessity of *explaining*, of ac-
counting for, the phenomena of the new community's
life. Strange things were happening and outsiders were
wondering what they meant. It was because the Spirit
had come—that is, the church had fully come into being
—that Peter was moved to speak; it was only for this
reason that he had anything to speak about. It is true
that his sermon consisted largely of a recalling of the
life, death, and resurrection of Jesus, but this event was
recalled in order to account for the existence of this
new community with its distinctive and intrinsically significant life. Without that "new creation," the creation
of the church, Peter would have had neither occasion to
preach nor text to preach on.

This same identity of the Spirit who inspires the preacher with the Spirit who constitutes the church is tacitly acknowledged when the author of I John, speaking of the "many false prophets," urges the church to "test the spirits to see whether they are of God" (4:1). For by what criteria can it test the spirits of its prophets and teachers except by its own Spirit, the Spirit of the church itself? To be sure, there may be more objective ethical tests to eliminate the charlatan or the more obviously self-deceived. But, in the last resort, the test must be spiritual. Unless the congregation finds the prophet's utterances calling to and answering to depths of its own shared experience, it can have no assurance that he is moved by the Spirit. Otherwise, it must conclude that he has a strange or evil spirit, or no spirit at all. His words must find its members at the deepest and most authentic level: in their awareness of their sin, of their dividedness and their finitude, of their need of forgiveness and healing, and of the reality of the salvation which God provides in Christ—the reality of the forgiving and healing love of God, which is being made constantly available through the community's own divinely given life. The writer to the Ephesians can speak of the prophet as God's gift to the church, but it is just as true that the prophet's own gifts have been conferred on him *through* the church and can be recognized as gifts of the Spirit only on that account.

But if preaching owes everything to the community, it also owes everything to the event. The message of the preacher, while it has been communicated to him

91

through the life of the church, was first given in some ancient happenings. The preacher, as we have so often reminded ourselves, is the preacher of the gospel—the good news of these happenings. The kērugma was at the beginning, as it is still, the proclamation of the life, death, and resurrection of Jesus, of the saving meaning that event proved to have, and of all that is still hoped for from it. But it is more than this. Just as preaching does not so much discuss or describe the life of the Christian community as actually to express and convey its concrete meaning, so preaching does more than recount and explain the ancient event. The Spirit makes the ancient event in a very real sense an event even now transpiring, and the preaching is a medium of the Spirit's action in doing so. In the preaching, when it is truly itself, the event is continuing or is recurring. God's revealing action in Christ is, still or again, actually taking place.

This character of preaching as being not merely a reporting of the event but itself a part of it is often brought out in the New Testament. In Rom. 1:16, Paul writes, "I am not ashamed of the gospel: it is the power of God for salvation." By the "gospel" Paul means, of course, the preaching; and his point is not simply that the *event* proclaimed in the preaching is the saving "power of God," but that the preaching itself participates in this "power." The preaching is an extending of the event itself, not merely of the knowledge of it. So also in I Cor. 1:21, Paul speaks of "preaching" as being the means through which God will "save those who believe." It is *Christ crucified and preached* who is "the power of God

92

and the wisdom of God." Similarly, in Luke 4:18 ff. Christ's quotation from the prophet Isaiah, "The Spirit of the Lord is upon me, because he has anointed me to preach good news to the poor," seems to make the preaching of the gospel an element in the gospel itself. This is even more clearly done in the words of Jesus to the disciples of John in Luke 7:22-23: "Go and tell John what you have seen and heard: the blind receive their sight, the lame walk, lepers are cleansed, and the deaf hear, the dead are raised up, the poor have good news preached to them."

The event with which the preacher is concerned is an ancient event which happened in Palestine in the first century, and it is very important that it be remembered as such. But it is not that only—it is happening still, or again and again, and one of the ways of its continual recurring is the preaching itself. Here is the final test of Christian preaching, if it be genuine preaching and genuinely Christian: Does it really convey the saving action of God? Just as God used the life, death, and resurrection of Jesus, so also, if in a subordinate way, is he using the preacher's preaching of that life, death, and resurrection as the medium of his power and love? Is Christ again saying, "Come unto me"? and, being even now lifted up, is he drawing us to him? Do we actually see him dying for our sakes, and indeed at our hands? Is he showing himself, even to us, alive after his passion, raised for our redemption? Insofar as preaching is failing, here is the primary point of its failure—not that it fails to be learned enough, or entertaining enough, or brief enough, or "modern" enough, but that God's power and action are not being effectively communicated in it. This is the primary point of failure, because in failing here, preaching is failing to be preaching at all. A man is expressing his opinions, true or false, interesting or uninteresting, about matters important or unimportant. But God is not acting. Something is being said, but nothing is taking place. The judging and saving event of Christ is not recurring. The Spirit, the "glorious might" of God, is not present.

What we are affirming here is the sacramental nature of preaching. For the double relationship with the event to which we are now pointing as belonging essentially to preaching constitutes also the essential nature of the Eucharist. It is right to see in the Lord's Supper a memorial of Christ; what is being done is "in remembrance" of him, and to fail to remember him would be to miss the whole meaning of the sacrament. But this is not to say that the act of remembering *is* the whole meaning. Whatever their profession may be, no large body of Christians regards the Lord's Supper as being only a memorial, a reminder of something that happened long ago. Something is now happening; the ancient event is now taking place. What God did in Christ he is now doing. Thus it is with the sacrament. So it is also with the preaching. This is the meaning of the Spirit, who takes Christ's words and God's deed—and lo, the words are again being spoken, the deed is again being done.

If someone asks, "How can these things be?" one must answer that this is the single ultimate and inescapable miracle in Christianity—this contemporaneity of

94

what has long since happened, this actuality in the present of what is also remembered in the past. This is the miracle of the Resurrection. But although it cannot be explained and is therefore a miracle, it constitutes the very existence of the church and is therefore indubitable. It is the miracle of the church's own distinctive life, and sacraments are real sacraments and preaching is real preaching only if this miracle is being wrought in them.

NOTES

1. I am indebted to my friend, the Rev. George F. Woods, of Downing College, Cambridge, for calling my attention to this passage. It is found in *Works* (London: Printed for J. Richardson, 1762; probably reprinted for G. Moreton, 1893), VII, 186.

2. Chicago: Willett Clark and Company, 1936. The several passages quoted are used with the permission of Harper & Brothers, the present publishers.

3. New York: Charles Scribner's Sons, 1950.

4. *A Cambridge Bede Book* (New York: Longmans Green & Company, 1936), p. 15.

5. *The Study of the Bible* (Chicago: University of Chicago Press, 1937), pp. 103 ff. Copyright 1937 by the University of Chicago. The quotation is with the permission of the University of Chicago Press.

6. A fuller discussion of this principle of interpretation will be found in my small book *Criticism and Faith* (New York and Nashville: Abingdon Press, 1952), especially the final chapter, "Historical Criticism and Preaching."

7. Chicago: Willett Clark & Company, 1937.

8. See the very helpful article "The Christian Teacher in the First Century," by Floyd V. Filson, *Journal of Biblical Literature*, LX, 317-28.

9. Norman Foerster and John M. Steadman (Boston: Houghton Mifflin Co., 1923).

10. *The Christian Century*, LXIII, 985 ff.